GLIMPSE OF DREAMS

RHYTHM PUBLICATION

ISBN 979-888546229-7

To those who participated in it, and who will read it.

Contents

Contents

Naveena Bhashini.J

Hello, this is Naveena Bhashini from Neyveli. I am currently working as a corporate professional and I have completed B.tech in BioTechnology stream. I started writing short glimpses from school days when I got a chance to write quotes on the school bulletin board every day and continued till now. I always felt like nothing is much more joy than my writings speared through one's heart. Sharing my mind through pen and paper and get connected with others through my writings.

FOLLOW ME ON INSTAGRAM - *@Bhashys_innerthoughts*

1. Things I'm Proud Of

I can smile even if I'm standing at my last chance to live,
I can sleep well even if I know what is waiting for me in the morning,
I can rebuild myself even if you break me tons of time,
I can save my energy instead of wasting it in worthless past,
I can control my thoughts by stopping them from wandering around the future plans,
I can pay my bills and won't need someone to pay mine,
I can take my own decision and don't need to give up my deciding authority to someone,
I can style myself as I wish even though I'm under body-shaming insults,
I can travel the world myself and don't need for a company as I m bold enough to protect myself,
I can fill your tummy with heartfelt food and you don't need to wait for a takeaway,
I can be your light in your scariest night so that you don't need to feel lonely,
I can support you emotionally and financially so that you don't need to own all burdens,
I can be your all in all so that you can trust me blindly,
I can give you my shoulder all the time so that you can share your grief and anger,
I am proud of myself for being a HUMAN.

- Naveena Bhashini. J

2. One Lost, But Now Found

I thought you are all mine and trusted you blindly,
Dreaming the day of getting together in front of thousands of eyes,
I never had a dream of moving apart and never ever thought that your soul-soothing words
Will turn into this disgusting language.
I was spending my days analyzing mistakes from my end
That is what made you leave me.
It took me almost a year to realize that I have truly lost you
And you are not mine now and hereafter.
Then I opened my eyes and heart to look at what is really worth?
Finally, I came to know what really worth is…ME
I found that I don't lose love, I lost me in loving you
I found that I own the decision of my life, I should choose what suits me
I should choose what my next plant in life would be.
Who left me is not my problem absolutely
And I still can choose who wants me.
I have my life, I have a long way to go
I can decide how to live my life.
Life pushed me to move on and start again.
So I found now what I have lost once.

- Naveena Bhashini. J

Narayani Joshi

An expressive, deliberate, and observatory person, Narayani has the ability to express her views in an exquisite manner that is simple yet heart-touching.

FOLLOW ME ON INSTAGRAM - ***@the.nariko***

3. Dreams - The Fall And Rise

Often I cry out thinking about the storms
Which swept away my dreams in one rush
The storms of misery and el-doubt which made my dreams
Go down the drain.
I remember the storms coming in from an open window
And taking away my life and my dreams
Almost breaking my fragile soul like glass
And all I could do was to lay on my cold floor
Just to witness blood and tears come out from my eyes.
But as they say, "After a storm comes a bright sun"
After a long wait it came, filling me with life
And I molded a new life inside me
A new dream, a new me and a new soul
Were given rise by my shattered heart.
Dreams give you joyful and heart wrenching experiences
And what you have to do is to endure the pain
While the storm is on the onset and
Enjoy the bliss when the Sun knocks on
Your broken yet open window.

- Narayani Joshi

Vanshika Garg

If you are chatty

If you love to write and read

If you love to be dramatic sometimes

Then Hi-Five!

FOLLOW ME ON INSTAGRAM - *@Vanshika0702*

4. Secret Prayer

You know him better
everyone used to say
But I know the truth
because I used to pray
Pray to have a chance
to know your soul
Not only a part of you
but as a whole
But that vulnerability
makes me weak
Deep into my heart
something used to tweak
And I am not ready
to let my walls down
I know it will hurt
and later I will frown
So it's better to pray in silence
that all your dreams come true
May you keep shining
and win every battle that comes through!

- Vanshika Garg

5. Raise A Toast

Oh Girl !!
You clicked ten pictures
and deleted nine of them
You stared at last one for ten minutes
and you deleted that too
You tried a dress
It fits you well
But you won't buy it
because it doesn't suit your skin color as you are not fair
You know what's unfair
"These insecurities"
My nose is too big
My legs are so thin
Oh my God! I must dig
and bury myself in
I can't be on stage
Up there they need a beautiful face
But I look too old for my age
and that's the problem in my case
These insecurities just make you weak
and your heart tweak
But don't you ever kneel down
Just look up and see that you are also wearing a crown
Stand up to them and say

that "I make my own way"
I can walk on any stage
and that too, at any age
I don't need someone with me to walk a mile
I can do that alone with a smile
And in this journey, by chance
by chance, you are having a bad day
that is getting you roast
then my girl, pour yourself a drink
and raise a toast !!

- Vanshika Garg

Shafrin

I am Shafrin pursuing my bachelor's in biochemistry. I strongly believe that words have the magic either to bring about war or peace and hence we must use them wisely.

FOLLOW ME ON INSTAGRAM - *@_.chandhini.__*

6. A Cosmic Dream An Unrequited Love Story

She was a cosmic beauty,
Made of Stardust and was filled with the luminescence
Of the Moon.
She was like the Andromeda Galaxy, bright and beautiful.
She was the Orion Nebula
In his darkest night.
Her eyes cherished the
Mysteries of the Marineris valley,
All her beauty revolved around the unfathomable heart
Of the Blackhole.
Her beauty was elusive for
His imperceptive eyes
And his callous heart.
Whose existence was not seen
But was felt.
Felt so deep that she was completely lost
one day.
- Shafrin

7. Cosmic Dream

Her body was a universe
Sparkling with erotic energy ;
As she danced across,
The Milkyway
While tracing the Spiral Galaxy of
pleasure.
The enormous energy
coiled within her could
Contract no more.
And exploded outward as
Her body convulsed
A thousand sun bloomed
As a wreath around her head fading her face, Time
stoped. As protons and
neutrons escaped from
Her parted-lips
She was in a wordless cry.
- Shafrin

Sandra Prasanth

Hi! I am Sandra Prasanth. I am a student of Marian College Kuttikkanam. I live in Kerala with my parents. I love writing poems, reading books and listening to music. If you enjoyed reading my poem, do follow and support me on instagram.

FOLLOW ME ON INSTAGRAM - ***@serene_wordss***

8. The Monster

When the clock struck twelve
The lights went dull
And I could smell
The thing that swell
The doors went jarred
And I was scared
Noises aloud
Clear and around
It grabbed me from behind
And dragged my hand
I yelled, I cried
But nobody hied
"Hey boy wake up"
I came to my sense
A dream was that
I thought and sat
Round I looked
Around me was light
A day that was bright
I looked above, below
And stood steady and slow
Again closed my eyes
Few minutes passed
Then opened my eyes and gasped

Watching the empty park
Turning dark
Then I saw it
Even though lights dim
It came close
And flew away
This time not alone,
It took me

- Sandra Prasanth

Vikram Singh Parihar

Working in the banking sector for the last 9 years, keen to share emotions through writing from early school days and with the pace of time polishes to express the different emotions through different words to express.

FOLLOW ME ON INSTAGRAM - ***@Parihar29***

9. Firm Hands

Trembling is a way to handle emotions
Thoughts are a base to make words
Tackling acts makes worldly affairs
Tougher hands makes generations
Uttering words can't change scenarios
Unspoken truth can't stand for others
Untold memories can't built histories
Unshaken hands can't bear lies
Venom is the cure to the venom itself
Vermin to society mirror of world itself
Vandalism of society taking care itself
Victory to handle folded hands itself
With hands to make the wounds of war
With hands to handle the wounds of war
With hands firm the righteous way too far
Withheld hands always firm for a needy hour
- Vikram Singh Parihar

10. Melody

It's the perception which makes it smoothening
It's the moment which makes it happening
It's the mood which validate the swing
It's the peace which is striving hard for coming
Combination of sounds leads heart for happiness
Combination of colours seek sight for happiness
Caring for others creates place for happiness
Comforting self a vent of havoc for happiness
Trusting eyes are needed for consultation
Thanking attitude is needed for self realization
Thoughtful doubts are mediator for stabilization
Twinkling eyes are remedy for inner satisfaction
Time is caretaker of melody of memories
Truth is eye-opener of melody of allegations
Trust is firm base of melody of happiness
Tough is soft melody of desires of carelessness

- Vikram Singh Parihar

M Lithei Nyam

I'm M.Lithei Nyam Phom, residing in a beautiful North Eastern State of India known as Nagaland. I'm a working woman who is also a book lover and writing serves as my hobby. Through this column, I would love to explore more of myself and my interest in writing poems and stories.

FOLLOW ME ON INSTAGRAM - ***@LITHEI NYAM PHOM***

11. Chosen Womb

Heaven must've agreed your womb to be my home.
Bore me gracefully till your beautiful body is disfigured.
How hard it must've been, unfathomed sleepless nights.
Everyone admired your blessed womb.
You gleefully pinned down the pain.
You weren't afraid for birthing was never a trial.
Fearfully and bravely labored the pain.
My first superhuman, superhero, super mom.
Kisses to the hands that feed me and the lap that rest my head.
You're my best friend all along.
Your un-numbered sacrifices and goodness fill me.
From your womb till my tomb,
I'll always owe you, dear mamma.
The world has a lot to point at you. Let them!
For my heart knows your womb's my first home.
The abode of love.

- M Lithei Nyam

12. Undress

NAKED NOT UNCLOTHED!
LEARN TO SEE HER SOUL'
DARE TO SEE THE PAIN.
THEY'RE GLISTENING LIKE THE RAINBOW;
EACH SHOT IS A PIECE THAT'S GIVEN AWAY.
EMPTIED! THE RAYS PASS THROUGH....'
STOP WONDERING!...
THESE WOUNDS ARE THE EMOTIONS CRAVED BENEATH THE SKIN.
TOUCH NOT WITH THE BODY,
BUT WITH YOUR GLIMMERING EYES.
IT'S A CONSCIOUS TOO DEEP.
A BARE HANDS WON'T FEEL.
FOR YOU HAVE TO FIX YOUR BODY, MIND, AND HEART TO UNDRESS HER.
FOR SHE'S THAT NAKED TRUTH, LONGING TO BE DEVOURED IN.

- M Lithei Nyam

Aswathy U K

I am neither an accomplished writer nor an accomplished poet. Writing is a means of catharsis for me to sort through my emotions and memories.

FOLLOW ME ON INSTAGRAM - ***@aswathyuk***

13. Spurned

Like cotton seeds being dispersed in the wind, I love freely and without restrictions.
I am not perfect but nobody is, for the beauty of a person lies in his imperfections,
In his willingness to rectify his flaws, in his eagerness to try again, and I am trying !!!
I am trying my best every single day.
But it's not enough, it's never enough, because it's so easy, to resent me, to ignore me, to forget me;
For I loved someone with my whole heart once but I wasn't enough.
My love was valueless and thrown away and I got shallow words and actions in return.
I don't know what or whom I am searching for except for a way to rewrite the memories.
Spluttering and flickering the flames might be but I will return as an inferno to ravage through the obstacles in my path.

- Aswathy U K

Sanskaar Shetty

Hey guys, I'm a budding writer, just recently started off with my blog, and side by side I am also pursuing majors in economics, and still haven't figured out what's best for me. Just like any other average teenager.

FOLLOW ME ON INSTAGRAM - *@sanskaarshetty*

14. With you and only you

From what lies at the end of the horizon,
To the secrets of the oceans,
I wanna explore all these secrets,
But with you, and only you.
From what bounty the jungles hide,
To the science behind places like a stone hedge,
I wanna discover all these secrets,
But with you, and only you.
From the treasures hidden in the feelings of animals,
To the warmth of the sun,
I wanna enjoy all of them,
But with you, and only you.
From the feeling of being embraced by love,
To the feeling of being protected,
I wanna feel all of them,
But this time not with you, but rather from you.

- Sanskaar Shetty

Devdas The Poet

He is an avid rhymer & a spontaneous poet, who is often mused by anyone or anything that evokes an emotion in him. It can be from the faintest of smiles to the brightest of lights.

FOLLOW ME ON INSTAGRAM - *@devdasthepoet*

15. Mask

We all hide behind a mask
Our skeletal remains
Fake faces & true disdain
I think it's cause
We are torn between
Having to wear the mask
Or brandish the face we try
Immeasurably to conceal
Often left wondering
To be or Not to be...
- Devdas The Poet

16. Scald

A journey undertook
To reach where I wanted
I reflect to ponder
On the sins, I committed...
As I sit here
The flames of penitence
Scald me more
Then the embers of Hell
I had to walk upon...
- Devdas The Poet

17. Anger

Blinded by fury
We often scream
Each battling their own demons
Only they can see
These demons rest in our heads
Goading us closer to the edge
Confusing us to believe
That they manifest
In our own kind too
We begin to suspect,
These demons are wary of them
Know they will not stop
Until we're dead...
- Devdas The Poet

Vipra Kohli

Vipra is currently pursuing her 2nd professional year as a medic in Maharishi Markandeshwar Medical College and Hospital, Himachal Pradesh (India). She values her surroundings and is like an undying weed whose explosive power is awe-spring. She believes that every individual has their own spark in the same way she is also full of mystic shine and shade. She is curious to understand each new thing she catches on to and has an artistic temperament. Vipra believes that happiness and opportunities are perfectly harmonized with our very own karma. She thrives on the fact that people who are graced with the gift of sight, cannot un-see the truth and dwell in the darkness. Whether it is mixed media, digital, or assemblage, she seeks to merge experiences into unified painterly forms, whether one may see intensification, clarification, and interpretation of numerous forms and believes that everyone is blessed with lion-hearted courage, waiting to be explored!

FOLLOW ME ON INSTAGRAM - *@kohli_vipra*

18. KARMA- What You Sow, Is What You Reap!

Karma, oh my! My companion
I glom with delight and dodge with connections.
Enjoy the days when I had a lot of luck.
I Felt attacked when the same happened to me.
And had the listing that got mixed up.
Karma, you are the law of the universe.
I am a shy and timid person, believe it or not.
Calm me with wisdom, and this small favor
Will take me along the path to becoming a new man.
Fabricate a friendship band for me too.
Simply guide me on how to convince myself
I also want to be the best without regrets
I am not scoundrel karma, trust me.
Before I go over the edge, I'd like to say a few words.
Just show me how to connect and transform my ordinary into amazing.
We humans realize, you have a decent heart
You treat everyone equal
Though, we speak to you in accordance with our craft.
Our sense of urgency and our aura
Believe me, when I say that I will not follow in the footsteps of others.
Believe me, my friend, I won't bluff again
But will work hard to make you my joy

Strive hard to make you my glee
And convince you to join our coalition.
You're portrayed as a powerful and frightening figure.
And it is only to your generosity that we have been able to construct our castle.
We people are aware that when we deceive a soul, the bricks fall away.
As a result, we are left with a handful of sand and tragedy.
And end up criticizing you without realizing it, it was our fault.

- Vipra Kohli

Rajesh Manna

Rajesh Manna is a corporate employee with a taste of creativity. He loves to write poems and thought-provoking quotes during his leisure. Blogger and Youtuber are his other designations apart from the one given by his employer. He loves to write on inanimate objects and tries to connect them to living things

FOLLOW ME ON INSTAGRAM - ***@Unsung_fable***

19. Not A Horror Story

Not a Horror Story
An eerie sound pierced the dark woods
as Mary stood Infront of a rustic cabin
Her dog was brave yet alarmed
that made it bark at every strange usual entity.
The surrounding was still yet chaotic
As the clouds covered the scarlet moon
with a deep sigh, Mary took a stride
and the dog followed her as a petrified soldier from behind
The thatched window slapped each other
as the chilly gale knocked them
and the unbidden guests entered the main hall
The entry door slammed as the savage breeze charged
Like the daylight clearing through the night sky
the faint moonlight gleamed through the broken glass
unveiling the indoor, illuminating the dark
As If the time has paused everything in the neighborhood
a broken chair sat immobile accompanied by a portrait
The lady in the sketch had a grin on her face
with lovely eyes and cascade hair
She stood there staring at the picture
and the dog couched for a nap
Suddenly, the wind slowed down
and a sweet scent filled the room

She fell asleep near the dog as the silence prevailed
recalling the days of a hot summer night
when Granny sang her tales of fairies and witches akin
As she opened her eyes, she found herself in bed
and a ray of light brightened making the room lit again
nothing was the same except her and the dog gazing at her with a smile.

- Rajesh Manna

Roneeca Brajasundar Sahu

I am a working professional, I write more inspirational quotes, sometimes emotional, love quotes. I think writing can express a few things in a better way that cannot be spoken.

FOLLOW ME ON INSTAGRAM - ***@roneeca8***

20. Still Keeping My Silence

Silence, which also means there
is a lot to say sometimes,
however the situation is not favorable to say,
I have been seeing violence taking place
at times,
but have to be silent because
could not find a way to solve this,
I will be seeing how some people will hurt others,
still have to be silent as my words don't
bring any changes to their life,
why the girl child has to be aborted
after these many years of Independence?
no proper action for this and I have to be
silent as majority always wins,
Why is the dowry system not banned?
girl's family sacrifices a lot and again being
silent is only the option,
Why few girls are not safe in the Country?
being knowing the reasons, can't raise voice
and have to be silent,
If it is right to speech, then why always the world wins
and an individual keeps quiet?
Why? why? Is the important question,
but I have to be silent as this world is very rude.

- Roneeca Brajasunder Sahu

21. If Time Could Stop

If the time is stopped at the moment,
It would cause uncertainty about
the future,
there will be no harm to the
Mother Nature,
the sufferings of the people will be paused,
the violence going on in many places
will come to an end,
happy moments will be captured forever,
children can cherish the golden days of their life,
time brings many unexpected things, so I wish if it is
stopped for a moment, then it should bring loads of
happiness, peace, success, and good fortune to
all the living beings on this marvelous planet.

- Roneeca Brajasunder Sahu

Vidhyasree. M

Being a 2nd year student of Dentistry, I turn to dancing Bharatanatyam, art and writing poems to rejuvenate. Writing has always been an amazing medium for me to share and express my thoughts and emotions.

FOLLOW MY BLOG - ***https://vidhyasree.home.blog/***

FOLLOW ME ON INSTAGRAM - ***@vidhyasthoughts***

22. Hope

A mist of doubt enveloped
Blurring the eyes and thoughts.
The memories made; away they galloped
Dreams & wishes made for the future were lost.
Hope and pray was all that could be done,
The gallop of memories, had now, changed to a run
But suddenly appeared the scorching sun-
Bringing the light which brought back the joy and fun.
The mist had disappeared
And gone were the days which were dreaded and feared.
The patches of doubt were trimmed and sheared,
For the beautiful future, they were geared.
- Vidhyasree. M

23. You

You're not a bane, you're never a burden,
About that, you should never be confused.
To be happy, sad, or anxious is just human,
But your emotions aren't something for them to be misused.
You're not asking for more,
You don't have to compromise
Your heart isn't meant to be torn,
By all the people to whom you've been nice.
Only you can love yourself-
In this life which is a maze,
Be your bold & beautiful self,
And the rest will fall into place.

- Vidhyasree. M

Sakura Koner

A biologist in the making, believing science can save lives and art can save souls, a dreamer without context, old soul in a young person

FOLLOW ME ON INSTAGRAM - *@bohemian_misanthropist*

24. My Mother

My mother reserves the best china for guests and us
She tells me she does not want to risk bringing them all out
Lest they break
"They are fragile, you see. Must not stress them."
But I have known her for as long as she has known me
I know she does disregard herself
Teaches me to be independent
But seeks refuge in others decisions
I know she takes the ugliest coffee mug
The torn placemat
The broken coaster
I know she had dreams
And the talent to fulfill them
I know she can rebel
Fight the world for the injustices
For herself
But I don't know what destroyed her confidence
I don't know what reduced her strength
Undermined her capabilities
I don't know when she ceased to be a lioness
Settled for less
Sedimented into banality and mediocrity
I don't know when she lost her voice
Was it when she screamed herself hoarse

At the chores, my father leaves undone
Was it when she was whisked away to a faraway family
Unknown and strange to her
Never having been asked once
Was it when she left her job
Confined herself to the kitchen
I don't know when the fire was doused
But sometimes I wonder if I know the culprit
Maybe I live and laugh with them
Maybe I have become them!

- Sakura Konar

Rhythm Thakur

She is Rhythm Thakur pursuing medical science and is a great lover of literature. She believes in penning down her emotions and is always up for the manifestation. She has goals in life and has all the more passion to accomplish them.

FOLLOW ME ON INSTAGRAM - ***@rhythm._.thakur***

25. Enlightening Heartbreak

I was sitting on a pyramid looking out for the love.
It got broken with no well-guarded interior but with you being so rough.
My hopes got shattered and my idea of inclination came to an end.
You could have proven me right but you chose to go with the words uttered by my friends.
They used to warn me to come down as they could foresee the future.
I was so sure not to get broken that today I can't even get help with any of the sutures.
No wounds could be seen to anyone out there physically.
But what about the unseen torture I have been fighting with mentally?
You could have been so outspoken when I just started to get a hold of you.
You were having multiples of chances to show me that it's not all true.
I wonder how you could be so heartless despite the fact that I handed over my heart to you.
How you could be so blind not to see my value?
But since this is a fact that I have loved you with all the purity.
Then there must be someone waiting for the same love with all the more surety.
One heartbreak is not going to decide my destiny.
I will keep on searching for my forever love even if there is no guarantee.
Love is still a beautiful essence for me. And this time my heart is no hurry.
I will probably get the love I have always desired for.
From today onwards I have all the time to explore.

- Rhythm Thakur

26. Old School Loving

Love each and every bit of him holding his soul in your arms.
Make him feel the beauty of your affection without any terms.
Treat him like you have decided to walk on a journey with a fixed destination.
Fight with no intentions of hurting him respecting the value of his expectations.

Don't try to bind him, set him all free.
You will find him undoubtedly loving you only.

Trust him with all his words and promises.
He will love you for sure ignoring all of your blemishes.

Give all of the pure love you have in your heart.
Make him feel wanted and special from the very start.
- Rhythm Thakur

Riya Kaushik.

She is Riya Kaushik, currently pursuing her bachelor's degree in English literature, and is driven by passion and hard work to accomplish each and every goal of her life. She is just 17 years old by age and truly devoted to entrepreneurship. She is a soul who attracts each and everybody by the charm of her nature of writing. She has fixed goals in life and she is walking on the pathway of manifesting them one by one.

FOLLOW ME ON INSTAGRAM - ***@the_riya_kaushik***

27. A Broken Heart Acquites.

With every blink of an eye, the sight I took
Reminds me of all your brightest and darkest Looks.
All those moments dumped deep in my heart
Definitely pinches me, but I forgive with all the grudges apart.
All I was left with lots of baseless promises and a wretched soul
Every second passed, I felt I am no anymore a part of my whole.
From us both, love was vast and disputed were mild
Suddenly that castle of love fell, accidentally killing the hidden child.
Purity and selflessness were from both
Moving together with dedication was our most rigid oath.
Didn't even realize, when this golden bond failed
Still in my heart, as an absolute, you are hailed.
Dear, wipe those tears and manifest that toothy smile
We traveled long, let's stop and breathe for a while.
Whatever happens, pragmatically, let it go
We will be better strangers to one another than being a foe.

- Riya Kaushik

Jagrit Saini

He is Jagrit Saini who is currently pursuing his B.Tech. He is a writer and an admirer of literature who wants to explore the beauty of literature through his pen. He always seeks improvement and keeps running on the path of obstacles to achieve his ultimate goal.

FOLLOW ME ON INSTAGRAM - ***@jagrit_saini_js***

28. The Unconditional Love

Wild and dark as I was, nothing ever mattered to me
running in the forest as I were a king, I never learned the importance of my heart safeguard
And every time I fell, I found those two hands always ready to pick me up
But my pride never valued her importance
At every stage of life, it was that one heart constantly beating for me
No matter how I treat her, she always brings me back from the edge
Lost in the land of unknowns, I always tend to abandon her
But she was always there no matter if I was asking or cherishing her presence or not
And as human greed never satisfies, I constantly push myself to have someone who could love me more World being world, every time all I got was one more scar to my already wounded soul
It was then I realized her love but was it too late to apologize was all I thought
Maybe my greedy soul was never able to understand her selfless love
Embracing me in her arms all she said was that she was never angry and just hurt
That was the time I realized that it's just a mother who can love you endlessly
It's the power of her love that can forgive every mistake without atonement for the sin.

- Jagrit Saini

29. The World Through Different Eyes

Well, infliction of pain is damn easy.
But what about making someone free?
Don't you want to look out for a better way to help the needy?
Can't you save them from the eyes of the greedy?
What about putting efforts to make them chin up?
Could you please try to prioritize and keep them at the very top?
Don't you want to become a crystal of clarity?
Would you really mind helping them to face the reality?
- Jagrit Singh

Leeharika Jindal

Leeharika Jindal is a 19 years old daughter of Mr. Parveen Jindal and Mrs. Anju Jindal. She is a literature student pursuing a Bachelors's degree in English Honours from Manav Rachna International Institute Of Research and Studies. She is a lively girl with a buoyant personality who is as distinct and unique as her name. She aspires to become a writer because someone else's words have changed her life in some way, and she hopes that one day her words will do the same for someone else.

30. Make yourself your own muse

Self-love is not a full stop at the end of a statement,
Neither it's a final destination down the pavement,
Rather it's an expedition, where after each comma
a beautiful journey of self-exploration commences.
There is no need of going to doctors
asking prescriptions for medicines,
Just add a pill of self-confidence with a glass full of patience
along with capsules of happiness day and night in your own prescription.
Yes, you can be your own source of happiness
and the one responsible for your own well-being.
There will be days when it will be more difficult
than others to find aspects of yourself,
But that is the time when you must sit with yourself
and listen to your soul.
Know what your soul desires
and do not allow anyone other than you
to question your perception of yourself,
And that questioning should only be aimed at bettering yourself,
And not the one that is undermining your morale,
Because you are solely responsible for your own improvement.
When you love yourself for who you are without judgments and criticism,
and with ardency and of your own accord,

You can become the best version of yourself.
You have the opportunity to make a positive difference
in your own life every day.
Make the necessary adjustments,
Until you arrive at the point where you are most at ease with yourself.
Take advantage of every opportunity to boost your self-esteem,
Because it is what will stick with you through thick and thin.
Go get a happening life, Because I believe that life's ultimate objective
and meaning is to find happiness for yourself.

- Leharika Jindal

9 798885 462297

Printed by Libri Plureos GmbH in Hamburg,
Germany